DEADLY

>>>> Factbook: Mammals

Look out for the other DEADLY books:

OUT NOW:

Deadly Factbook Minibeasts: Insects and Spiders
Deadly Factbook Reptiles and Amphibians
Deadly Factbook Fish, Squid and Jellyfish
Deadly Factbook Bizarre Beasts
Deadly Activity Book
Deadly Brain Teasers
Deadly Colouring Book
Deadly Top Ten Activity Book
Deadly Doodle Book 1, 2, 3
Deadly Diaries
Deadly Detectives

BBC
EARTH

DEADLY

>>>>>

Factbook:
Mammals

Orion
Children's Books

First published in Great Britain in 2012 by Orion Children's Books
This edition first published in Great Britain in 2014 by Orion Children's Books
a division of the Orion Publishing Group Ltd
Orion House
5 Upper St Martin's Lane
London WC2H 9EA
An Hachette UK Company

1 3 5 7 9 10 8 6 4 2

Photo credits
1 © Getty Images; 2 © Getty Images; 3 © BBC; 12 © BBC 2010; 14 © Rosie Gloyns 2009
(from Deadly 60 Series 1); 15 © BBC 2009; 17 © BBC 2009; 18-19 © BBC 2009; 24 © BBC 2009;
28 © BBC 2010; 30 © BBC 2011; 34 © James Brickell (from Deadly 60 Series 1); 36 © BBC 2010;
37 © BBC 2010; 38 © BBC 2010; 39 © BBC 2009; 40 © BBC 2010; 42 © BBC 2009;
6-47 © Rosie Gloyns 2009 (from Deadly 60 Series 1); 48 © BBC 2009; 52 © BBC 2010; 56 © BBC 2010;
57 © BBC 2010; 58 © BBC 2010; 65 © BBC 2010; 66 © Charlie Bingham 2010 (from Deadly 60 Series 2);
68 © BBC 2010; 70 © BBC 2010; Shutterstock: 26 Jeff Banke;
Ardea: 10 François Gohier; 20-21 Jagdeep Rajput; 22 Steve Downer; 32 M. Watson;
33 M. Watson; 44 Ferrero Labat; 45 Tom and Pat Leeson; 50 M. Watson; 51 Jean-Paul Ferrero; 54 Mark
Carwardine; 55 Kenneth W. Fink; 60 Tom and Pat Leeson; 61 Adrian Warren; 62 M. Watson; 63 M. Watson;
64 Kenneth W. Fink; 69 Clem Haagner; 71 Karl Terblanche; 72 Suzi Eszterhaus; 74 Nick Gordon;
76 Bill Coster; 77 Hans and Judy Beste; 78 Pat Morris; Pascal Goetgheluck

Compiled by Jinny Johnson   Designed by Sue Michniewicz

A catalogue record for this book is available from the British Library.

Printed and bound in China

MIX
Paper from
responsible sources
FSC® C005748

www.orionbooks.co.uk

CONTENTS

WHAT IS A MAMMAL?

A mammal is an animal that has at least some hair on its body, is warm-blooded and has a four-chambered heart.

A female mammal has mammary glands and feeds her young on milk from her own body.

Most, but not all mammals, walk on 4 legs, but in sea-living species, such as whales and seals, the legs have evolved into flippers for swimming.

Mammals include animals such as cats, dogs, elephants, monkeys – and us!

There are believed to be more than 5,000 species of mammal in the world today.

BIGGEST and SMALLEST

Chapter 1

The **BLUE WHALE** is the biggest animal in the world today. It is also believed to be the biggest animal known to have lived on our planet.

It is even heavier
than the most enormous dinosaurs,
such as *Diplodocus* and *Argentinosaurus*.

A full-grown blue whale
weighs up to 180 tonnes.
Females can be up to 30 metres long – that's
about the same as 2 huge articulated lorries
parked end to end.

One reason that whales can grow so huge
is that they live in the sea and the water
supports their weight.

The blue whale's heart is the
size of a small car and can
you believe that its tongue
weighs as much as an elephant?

As you might guess, the blue whale gives birth to the world's biggest baby. A baby blue whale is 7–8 metres long when it is born – that's twice the length of an average car.

The blue whale baby drinks more than a bathtub of its mother's milk a day. It puts on an amazing 90 kilograms or so in weight every day – that's the same as 90 big bags of sugar.

There are two types of

AFRICAN ELEPHANT

– the bush or savannah elephant and the forest elephant. The bush elephant is the largest living land mammal. The biggest male ever weighed about 10 tonnes and stood 4 metres tall at the shoulder, but most are a little smaller.

The African elephant has bigger ears than any other animal. They help the elephant lose heat and keep cool in the African sun.

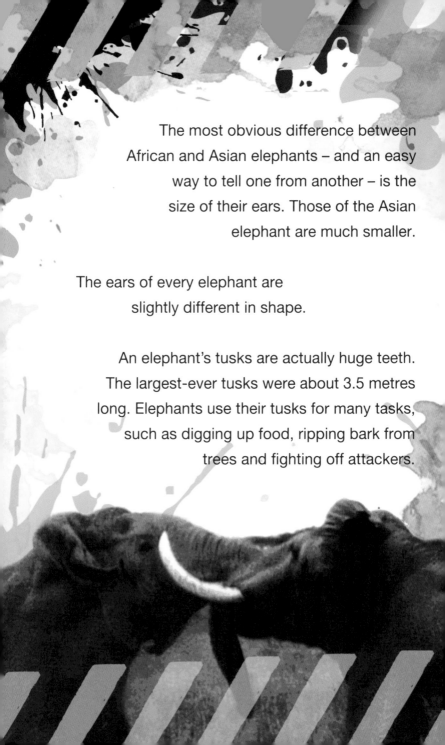

The most obvious difference between African and Asian elephants – and an easy way to tell one from another – is the size of their ears. Those of the Asian elephant are much smaller.

The ears of every elephant are slightly different in shape.

An elephant's tusks are actually huge teeth. The largest-ever tusks were about 3.5 metres long. Elephants use their tusks for many tasks, such as digging up food, ripping bark from trees and fighting off attackers.

BLUE WHALES and elephants need to eat vast amounts of food to keep themselves going. You might think the blue whale would eat giant prey, but it feeds by straining tiny shrimp-like creatures called krill from the water.

Each krill is only 6 centimetres long, but the blue whale can eat as many as 5 million of them a day. Fortunately there are billions of these little creatures living in the world's oceans. There are probably more krill than any other animal on earth and together they weigh more than all the humans in the world.

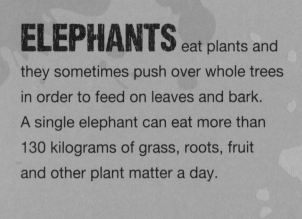

ELEPHANTS eat plants and they sometimes push over whole trees in order to feed on leaves and bark. A single elephant can eat more than 130 kilograms of grass, roots, fruit and other plant matter a day.

Imagine eating about 90 lettuces, 400 carrots and 250 apples and you'll get the idea!

The largest land carnivore – meat-eating mammal – is the **POLAR BEAR**.

A full-grown male weighs about 600 kilograms or so, more than 7 or 8 average people.

Not something you'd ever want to bump into!

The polar bear lives in the Arctic
and can survive in icy temperatures
of -37°C or less – that's much colder
than your freezer.

It has a sublime sense of smell and can sniff out
seal pups hidden in lairs beneath the snow from
as much as 2 kilometres away.

The bear also uses smell to find the holes
in the ice where seals pop up to breathe.
It watches patiently until a seal appears, then
leaps forward to drag it from the water.

The bear kills its prey
with a mighty bite to
the head.

The **TIGER** is the biggest big cat and an incredibly powerful beast. It's so strong that it can bring down prey twice its size and is truly a deadly hunter.

A tiger doesn't need to eat every day but does need to make a large kill every week or so. It can consume as much as 27 kilograms of meat in a night – that's like eating more than 200 hamburgers!

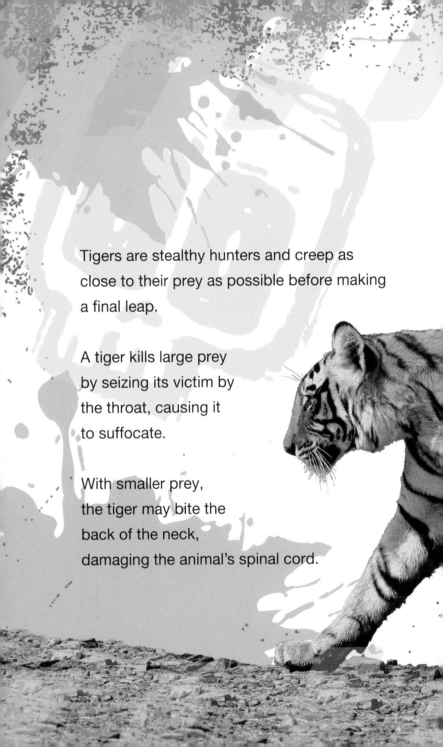

Tigers are stealthy hunters and creep as close to their prey as possible before making a final leap.

A tiger kills large prey by seizing its victim by the throat, causing it to suffocate.

With smaller prey, the tiger may bite the back of the neck, damaging the animal's spinal cord.

The largest tigers live in Siberia in the north of Russia. They can be up to 3.3 metres long and weigh a massive 300 kilograms. Even their claws are 10 centimetres long – longer than an adult human's fingers.

AWESOME!

One of the smallest of all mammals is a bat called the

BUMBLEBEE BAT

and as its name suggests, it's not much bigger than a bumblebee.

This tiny creature is about 3 centimetres long and weighs only 2 grams – less than a raspberry.It lives in caves in Thailand and is also known as Kitti's hog-nosed bat.

Despite its size, the bumblebee bat is a hunter. It eats insects, which it catches in mid-air or snatches from leaves. Like lots of bats, it finds its way in the dark and locates prey by using echolocation. The bat emits ultrasonic squeaks that bounce off objects in their path. The time it takes for the echo to return tells the bat how far away the object is and allows it to build a 'picture' of its surroundings and pinpoint prey. It can even tell whether an insect has a hard or soft body.

SPEED FREAKS

Chapter 2

The **CHEETAH**
is the speediest animal of all –
but only over short distances!
It can't keep up its high-speed chases
for very long.

This feline speedster can run at up
to 87 kilometres an hour for a few
hundred metres and can accelerate
to top speed in a few seconds.

INCREDIBLE!

A cheetah's speed is even more impressive
when you compare it to human runners.

Even the fastest Olympic athletes can
only manage speeds of about 37 kilometres
an hour in short bursts.

The **PRONGHORN** or American antelope is another incredibly fast-running mammal. It can run at 58 kilometres an hour for 6 kilometres or more – far longer than the cheetah. Pronghorns run fast to escape from deadly hunters such as coyotes and wolves.

The pronghorn's body has a number of special adaptations that help it run fast. It has long legs and strong muscles, but it also has a larger heart and lungs than most mammals its size. This means it can get lots of oxygen round its body quickly.

Mammals can swim fast too.
One of the champions is the
ferocious killer whale or
ORCA, which can swim at
up to 55 kilometres an hour.
That's much faster than
a champion Olympic
swimmer.

Killer whales
are some of the
deadliest of all
predators and have up to 56 sharp teeth,
which measure about 7.5 centimetres.

A killer whale cannot chew
but uses its teeth to seize its
prey and tear it to pieces.

KILLER WHALES use speed and
teamwork to catch their prey – they can even kill
other deadly hunters such as great white sharks.

Killer whales have been seen tipping seals off
ice floes into the waiting jaws of the rest of their
group, or pod.

The speediest sea lion is the

CALIFORNIA SEA LION,

which swims at 40 kilometres an hour
as it chases prey.

When searching for fish to eat,
the California sea lion dives deep and
can stay under for nearly 10 minutes
before coming up to take a breath.

The sea lion has special adaptations
that help it stay underwater for this long.
Its blood circulation changes when it dives
so that blood goes only to the most
essential organs, such as the brain
and heart, and it uses less oxygen.

Its heartbeat slows and this also saves oxygen.

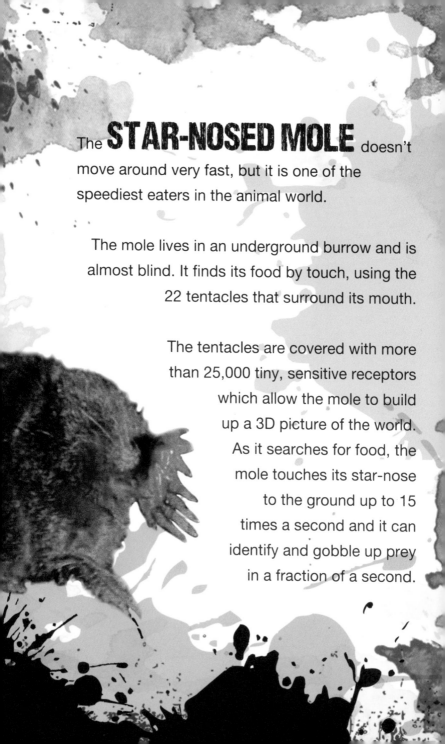

The **STAR-NOSED MOLE** doesn't move around very fast, but it is one of the speediest eaters in the animal world.

The mole lives in an underground burrow and is almost blind. It finds its food by touch, using the 22 tentacles that surround its mouth.

The tentacles are covered with more than 25,000 tiny, sensitive receptors which allow the mole to build up a 3D picture of the world. As it searches for food, the mole touches its star-nose to the ground up to 15 times a second and it can identify and gobble up prey in a fraction of a second.

DEADLY HUNTERS

Chapter 3

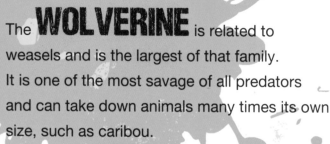

The **WOLVERINE** is related to weasels and is the largest of that family. It is one of the most savage of all predators and can take down animals many times its own size, such as caribou.

It is a scavenger too and its jaws are so strong that it can bite through the frozen flesh of animals it finds buried in snow. When prey is plentiful, the wolverine may bury food in the snow or store it in trees.

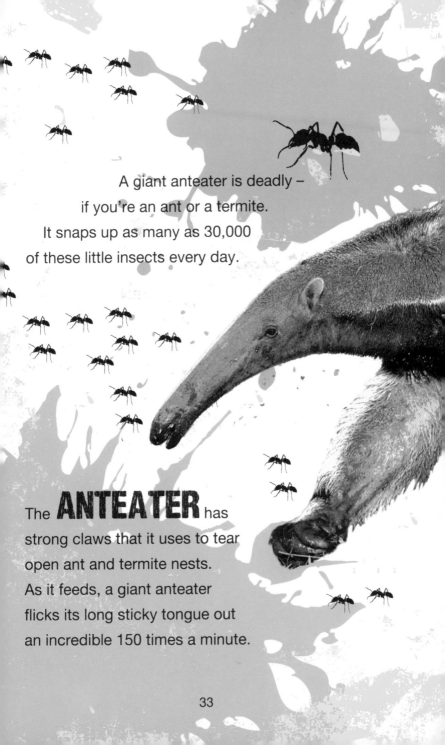

A giant anteater is deadly –
if you're an ant or a termite.
It snaps up as many as 30,000
of these little insects every day.

The **ANTEATER** has
strong claws that it uses to tear
open ant and termite nests.
As it feeds, a giant anteater
flicks its long sticky tongue out
an incredible 150 times a minute.

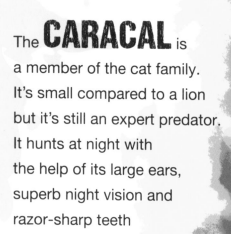

The **CARACAL** is a member of the cat family. It's small compared to a lion but it's still an expert predator. It hunts at night with the help of its large ears, superb night vision and razor-sharp teeth and claws.

And the caracal has an extra secret weapon. It can leap as high as 3 metres in the air to snatch a bird just as it's taking off – that's about as high as a basketball hoop.

The **STELLER SEA LION**

is the biggest sea lion and a fierce hunter. Although an adult male might weigh a tonne or more – about the same as a small car – it is fast and agile in the water as it hunts fish and other prey.

Female Steller sea lions are much smaller than males. They are only a half, or even a third, of the male's weight.

The **LYNX** is the largest cat in Europe but it hunts only at night and is rarely seen. It's fast, deadly and an amazing climber.

It's very cold in the areas where the lynx lives so it needs thick fur to keep it warm. Even its feet are furry so act like snowshoes to help it walk in deep snow.

The lynx's hearing and sight are excellent and it can spot a tiny creature, such as a mouse, from 75 metres away.

You don't usually think of **MONKEYS** as fierce hunters but the large ones, such as baboons, have long, sharp canine teeth.

Some hunt ground birds, small mammals and even fast runners such as Thomson's gazelle.

AFRICAN HUNTING DOGS

are very successful predators. They work in packs and the secret of their success is they can keep on running and running at speeds of up to 55 kilometres an hour until their prey is exhausted.

The dogs hunt as a team, often working to cut an animal off from its herd and drive it towards other members of the pack. They then gather for the kill, seizing the victim with their sharp-edged teeth to bring it down.

About 70 per cent of hunts are successful and the dogs share their kills with members of the pack – even those that haven't taken part in the hunt.

The **JAGUAR** is the largest cat in the Americas and the third largest of all cats, after the tiger and lion.

It is immensely strong but cannot run fast for long, so it needs to get as close as possible to its prey before making a final pounce.

It kills with a single bite to the victim's head or neck, piercing its skull with its deadly teeth.

Jaguars catch a wide range of prey including deer, capybaras, tapirs and peccaries.

They are good swimmers too and hunt in water as well as on land, catching caimans – a kind of crocodile – and tortoises and turtles.

A jaguar's jaws are so powerful that they can break turtle shells to get to the soft flesh inside.

LEOPARDS are skilful climbers as well as fierce predators. When a leopard makes a kill it sometimes carries its prey up into a tree to keep it away from lions and hunting dogs, or to store it for later.

DEADLY

This cat is so strong that it can climb while carrying prey heavier than itself.

BIZARRE BODIES

Chapter 4

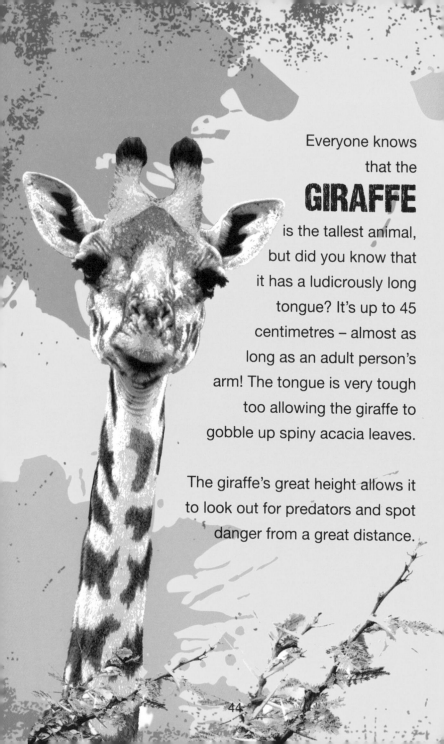

Everyone knows that the

GIRAFFE

is the tallest animal, but did you know that it has a ludicrously long tongue? It's up to 45 centimetres – almost as long as an adult person's arm! The tongue is very tough too allowing the giraffe to gobble up spiny acacia leaves.

The giraffe's great height allows it to look out for predators and spot danger from a great distance.

SEA OTTERS

live in the chilly waters of the North Pacific Ocean and need thick fur to keep them warm. A sea otter has what is probably the thickest fur of any animal with an amazing 100,000 hairs or more per square centimetre.

Sea otters sleep at sea, lying on their backs. They wrap themselves up in big pieces of seaweed, called kelp, so they don't get washed away as they snooze.

A hippopotamus can weigh 3 tonnes
or more, making hippos, along with rhinos,
the largest land animal after elephants.

HIPPOPOTAMUSES aren't very
hairy and they can burn easily in the hot African
sun. Fortunately the hippopotamus makes a
special sticky fluid in glands under the skin
and this acts just like a sunscreen.

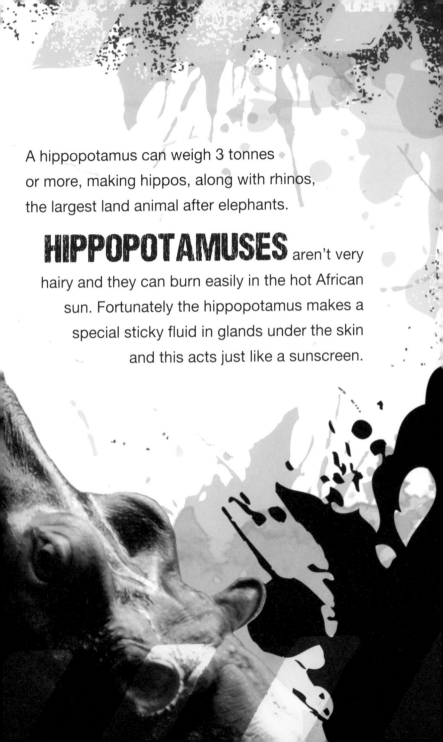

Hippopotamuses aren't predators – they feed mostly on grass – but they can be very aggressive and dangerous.

Males take part in fierce battles over territory and mates. They lunge at one another with their huge jaws gaping wide and sometimes cause serious wounds with their tusks.

The **NARWHAL** is a kind of whale.
The male has only 2 teeth but 1 of them
grows through the upper lip and
can be an astonishing 2.5 metres long.

No one knows quite why the narwhal has such
a long tooth but it may be for showing off to
female narwhals, who are impressed by
the size of a tooth.

A **SPOTTED HYENA**'s jaws and teeth are so strong that it can eat every scrap of its prey. It can even crunch through bones.

Spotted hyenas live and hunt in packs of as many as 80 animals. Females are bigger and fiercer than males and they're in charge – they lead the pack.

The
DUCK-BILLED PLATYPUS

doesn't look dangerous but it can be. The male has a sharp spur near each back foot and these spurs are linked to a venom gland.

It's thought that the spur is mainly used in battles with other males, or perhaps to pacify the female when mating, but if attacked, the platypus can stab this spur into its enemy to defend itself. The venom is strong enough to cause severe swelling and intense pain to a person.

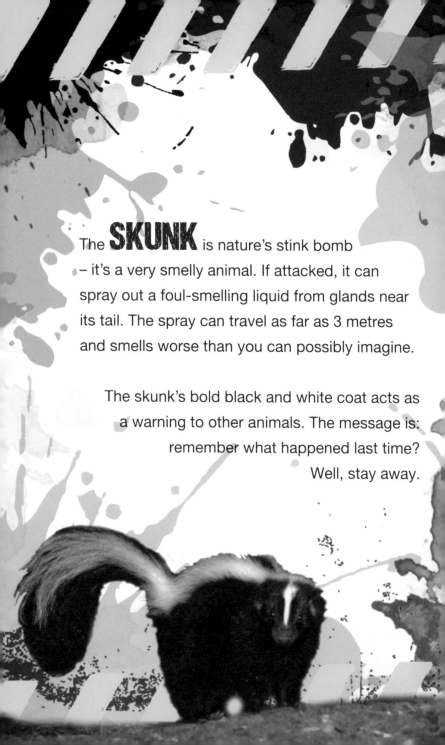

The **SKUNK** is nature's stink bomb – it's a very smelly animal. If attacked, it can spray out a foul-smelling liquid from glands near its tail. The spray can travel as far as 3 metres and smells worse than you can possibly imagine.

The skunk's bold black and white coat acts as a warning to other animals. The message is: remember what happened last time? Well, stay away.

SUPER SENSES

Chapter 5

One of the best night-time hunters is the **AYE-AYE**, a kind of lemur, which lives in Madagascar. It has huge ears for picking up the slightest sound, special eyes for seeing in the dark and an extra-long finger for extracting grubs from tree bark.

It's one of the weirdest creatures you'll ever see.

The
FENNEC FOX

is the smallest member of the dog family, but for its size it has the biggest ears of any meat-eating mammal. The ears are almost 15 centimetres long – the fox's body is only about 35 centimetres long.

The fox's large ears help it lose heat in the baking hot desert where it lives. They also help the fox hear the tiniest sounds of insect prey scuttling about on the ground.

The **ARCTIC FOX** also has keen hearing and can hear even the faintest squeaks of a lemming – its main prey – beneath the snow. The fox then tracks down its prey and digs it out with impressive speed.

Thick fur keeps the Arctic fox warm in temperatures colder than a freezer. In fact, it has the warmest fur of any mammal.

Like all bears, the **BLACK BEAR** has a highly developed sense of smell. It can smell carrion – animals that are already dead – more than 1.6 kilometres away.

Scent is also the way a female bear usually recognises her offspring.

BLACK BEARS are the least fussy about food of any of the bears.

They will eat everything from berries and nuts to the remains of a takeaway dinner.

AMAZING FEATS

Chapter 6

The **SNOW LEOPARD**

is a champion long jumper. This big cat has been seen making a leap of 15 metres. The Olympic long jump record is 8.95 metres.

The snow leopard's tail is up to 1 metre long and helps the cat balance as it leaps. The tail also helps the snow leopard keep warm in its cold mountain home. It wraps the tail round itself like a woolly scarf. Like all cats, the snow leopard is a predator and hunts animals such as wild sheep and goats.

CHIMPANZEES are among the few animals that use tools. They have been seen using stones to break large fruits into bite-sized pieces. And they use sticks to winkle termites out of their nests.

Did you know that chimps know how to cure tummy ache? They have been seen picking and eating leaves that local people know are a remedy for tummy troubles.

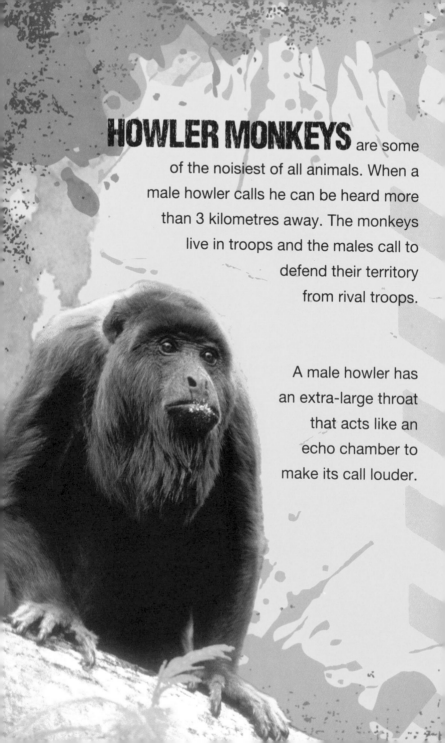

HOWLER MONKEYS

are some of the noisiest of all animals. When a male howler calls he can be heard more than 3 kilometres away. The monkeys live in troops and the males call to defend their territory from rival troops.

A male howler has an extra-large throat that acts like an echo chamber to make its call louder.

The huge **SPERM WHALE** dives deeper than any other whale. It plunges to at least 1,000 metres, maybe more, and stays there for over an hour. It dives to find its main food – deep-water squid. Before making a dive, the whale takes many deep breaths to build up as much oxygen as possible in its body.

The **GREY WHALE** is a champion migrator. It makes a round trip of about 16,000 kilometres each year, as it journeys between good feeding areas in the North Pacific to warmer waters farther south, where it mates and gives birth to young.

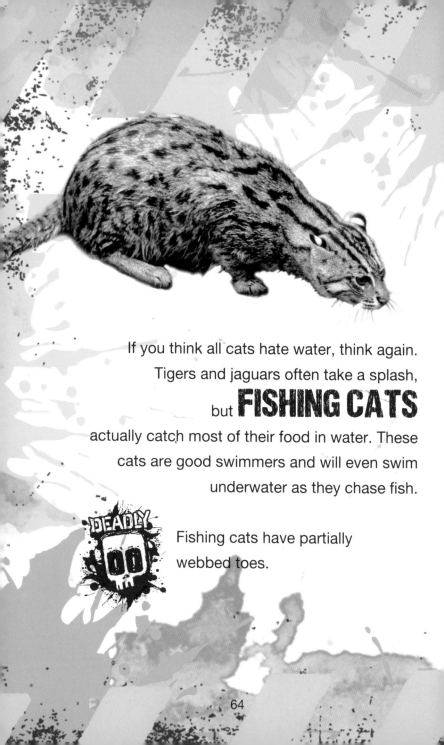

If you think all cats hate water, think again. Tigers and jaguars often take a splash, but **FISHING CATS** actually catch most of their food in water. These cats are good swimmers and will even swim underwater as they chase fish.

Fishing cats have partially webbed toes.

One of the champion tree-climbing cats is the

CLOUDED LEOPARD

which has large paws and long sharp claws to help it grip. It can even hang upside down as it climbs along branches. It also has extra-flexible joints on its rear ankles that help its feet turn, allowing the cat to climb down tree trunks head first.

The clouded leopard has the biggest canine teeth of any cat for its skull size. It usually hunts at night and preys on monkeys and birds in trees.

DEADLY

Did you know that only four cats can roar? They are the lion, tiger, leopard and jaguar.

All other cats can purr, but they can't roar.

FAMILY MATTERS

Chapter 7

LIONS are the only cats that live in groups. A lion family is called a pride and usually contains a number of females and their young and 1 or more adult males.

Lions in a pride hunt together and help look after each other's cubs.

MEERKATS are small, sharp-toothed carnivores which live in groups of adults and young. The group works as a team to protect each other and look after their young.

Lots of other predators, such as birds of prey, hunt meerkats so while most of the group are busy finding food, 1 meerkat keeps watch. If the look-out animal spots danger it makes an alarm call to tell the others to dive for cover. Meerkats also gang up to drive away enemies.

All the adults help to keep the young in the group well fed and bring them prey such as insects and scorpions.

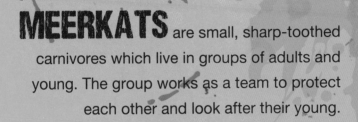

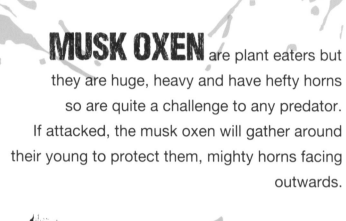

MUSK OXEN are plant eaters but they are huge, heavy and have hefty horns so are quite a challenge to any predator. If attacked, the musk oxen will gather around their young to protect them, mighty horns facing outwards.

Despite their bulk, musk oxen can run surprisingly swiftly. Male rivals charge one another at up to 40 kilometres an hour.

A human pregnancy lasts 9 months and an elephant carries her baby for 22 months. Like most mammals, humans and elephants are placental mammals. Their unborn babies are nourished inside the mother's body through a special organ called the placenta.

Marsupial mammals have a more primitive placenta and so a much shorter pregnancy – the Eastern quoll gives birth after a pregnancy of about 21 days. Marsupial young finish their development after birth, often in a pouch on the mother's body.

GORILLAS are the biggest of all the primates – the group that contains monkeys, chimps and us. A full-grown male can weigh twice as much as an adult man and is hugely strong and muscular.

Gorillas are peaceful plant eaters, but they can be fierce if disturbed and will fight to the death to defend their family.

FAVOURITE FOODS

DEADLY

Chapter 8

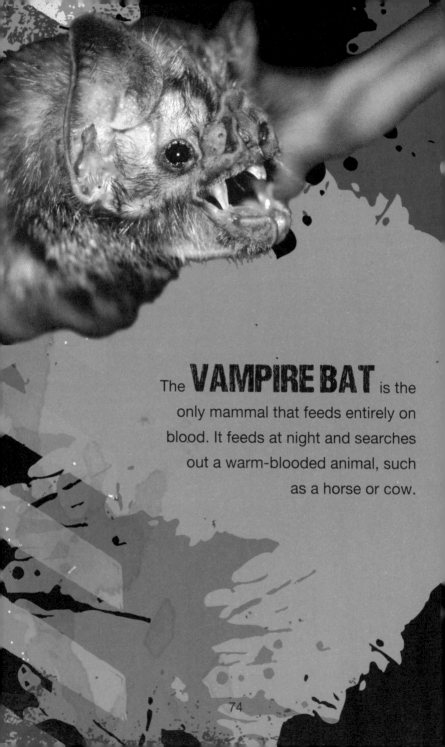

The **VAMPIRE BAT** is the only mammal that feeds entirely on blood. It feeds at night and searches out a warm-blooded animal, such as a horse or cow.

The vampire climbs up on to its victim, shaves away the hair from a patch of skin with its scalpel-sharp front teeth, and makes a small wound. It then laps up the blood as it flows from the wound – the bat's saliva contains a special substance that stops the blood clotting.

A vampire bat takes about a teaspoon of blood at each feed.

Vampires live in groups called colonies. If one of the colony hasn't managed to find a blood meal another bat will regurgitate some of its supper. Might not sound too good, but if you're hungry...

Despite its name, the
CRABEATER SEAL 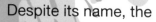 doesn't eat
crabs. Like the blue whale, it feeds on krill –
little shrimp-like creatures.

The crabeater seal eats about 20 kilograms
of krill a day, sieving them from the water
through its special teeth.

Like the Eastern quoll,
the **TASMANIAN DEVIL**
is a marsupial. A strong, fierce creature, it can
catch prey but usually feeds on carrion .

The devil has a powerful sense of smell that
helps it find food and it will devour the
rotting bodies of anything from insects to
wallabies. With its powerful jaws and teeth
it can chomp through tough skin, fur and
bones as well as flesh.

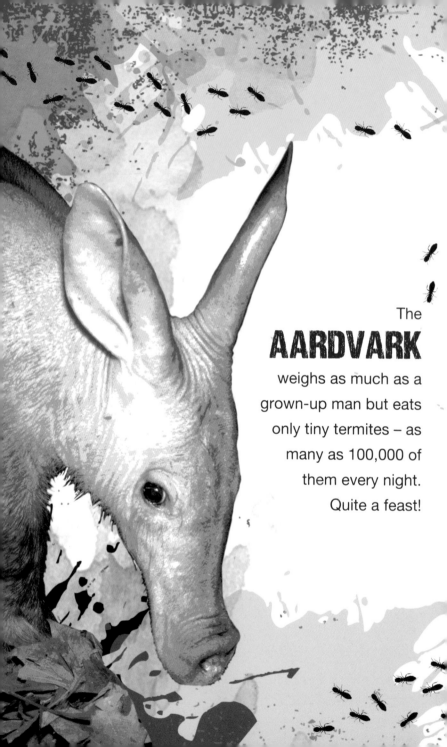

The
AARDVARK
weighs as much as a grown-up man but eats only tiny termites – as many as 100,000 of them every night. Quite a feast!

The aardvark's eyesight
is bad but it does have a great
sense of smell for sniffing out
its prey. It also has strong claws
for breaking into termite nests.

It pokes its long snout into the nest
and gathers large amounts of termites
with its sticky tongue, which measures an
extraordinary 30 centimetres. The aardvark
then crushes its insect meal with the broad teeth
at the back of its long jaws.

The aardvark's teeth are very unusual.
Unlike the teeth of most mammals they
have no roots or enamel coating. They keep
on growing throughout the animal's life.

Would you fancy a cobra for breakfast?

The **INDIAN MONGOOSE**
is so crafty and speedy it can manage to
catch and kill these deadly snakes.

The little mongoose seizes hold of the back
of the cobra's head to avoid getting bitten
by its deadly fangs.